What Now, Charlie Brown?

Selected Cartoons from
THE UNSINKABLE CHARLIE BROWN, Vol. I

Charles M. Schulz

CORONET BOOKS
Hodder Fawcett Ltd., London

Printed and bound in Great Britain for
Coronet Books,
Hodder Fawcett Ltd,
St. Paul's House, Warwick Lane,
London, EC4P 4AH
by Hazell Watson & Viney Ltd,
Aylesbury, Bucks

ISBN 0 340 16712 2

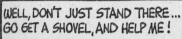

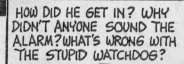

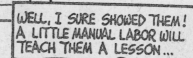

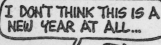

NEVER SET YOUR STOMACH FOR
A JELLY-BREAD SANDWICH UNTIL
YOU'RE SURE THERE'S SOME JELLY!

WELL, I LEARNED SOMETHING ABOUT JUMPING ROPE IN THE RAIN....

SOME JUMP ROPES **SHRINK**!

THAT VACUUM CLEANER SURE MAKES A LOT OF NOISE...

YOU'D MAKE A LOT OF NOISE TOO IF SOMEONE WERE PUSHING YOU ACROSS A CARPET ON YOUR FACE!

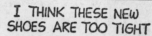

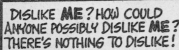

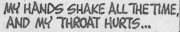

SEE WHAT YOU THINK OF THIS IDEA...

WHY DON'T WE TELL MOM THAT WE'RE SORRY ABOUT ARGUING OVER THE TV ALL THE TIME, AND PROMISE NEVER TO DO IT AGAIN?...THAT WAY, MAYBE SHE'LL FORGIVE US, AND BRING THE TV BACK INTO THE HOUSE..

YOU MEAN, COMPROMISE?

NEVER!

I THINK I'M STUCK WITH A BAD ALLIANCE!

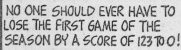

CLUMP
BUMP
FLUTTER

FLUTTER
BAM — FLUTTER
WHAM BUMP

KLUNK CLINK WHAM

I HOPE MY INSURANCE COVERS THIS SORT OF THING..

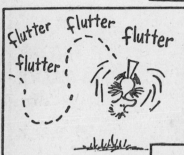

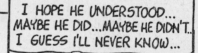

TRY TO STAY CALM....
I HAVE TERRIBLE NEWS!

DAD'S BEEN TRANSFERRED!
WE'RE MOVING TO A NEW CITY!

AAUGH!

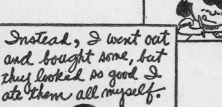

C'MON, LINUS, EACH OF US IS SUPPOSED TO SAY A FEW WORDS AROUND THE CAMPFIRE TONIGHT...

AS I STAND HERE TONIGHT FAR FROM HOME, I AM REMINDED OF THE WORDS FROM JEREMIAH "KEEP YOUR VOICE FROM WEEPING, AND YOUR EYES FROM TEARS;

FOR YOUR WORK SHALL BE REWARDED, SAYS THE LORD, AND THEY SHALL COME BACK FROM THE LAND OF THE ENEMY. THERE IS HOPE FOR THE FUTURE, SAYS THE LORD, AND YOUR CHILDREN SHALL COME BACK TO THEIR OWN COUNTRY."

INCIDENTALLY, HAVE ANY OF YOU EVER BEEN TOLD ABOUT "THE GREAT PUMPKIN"?

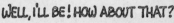

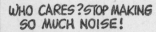

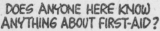

NOW, I THINK NO ONE WILL DENY THAT SPIRIT PLAYS AN IMPORTANT ROLE IN WINNING BALL GAMES..

SOME MIGHT SAY THAT IT PLAYS THE MOST IMPORTANT ROLE..

THE DESIRE TO WIN IS WHAT MAKES A TEAM GREAT..WINNING IS EVERYTHING!

THE ONLY THING THAT MATTERS IS TO COME IN FIRST PLACE!

WHAT I'M TRYING TO SAY IS THAT NO ONE EVER REMEMBERS WHO COMES IN SECOND PLACE!

I DO, CHARLIE BROWN... IN 1928, THE GIANTS AND PHILADELPHIA FINISHED SECOND. IN 1929, IT WAS PITTSBURGH AND THE YANKEES.. IN 1930, IT WAS CHICAGO AND WASHINGTON.. IN 1931, IT WAS THE GIANTS AND THE YANKEES.. IN 1932, IT WAS PITTSBURGH AND...

AND ANOTHER GREAT SEASON GETS UNDERWAY!

I DON'T KNOW ABOUT THIS NEXT BATTER, CHARLIE BROWN...HE'S PRETTY GOOD..

THAT'S RIGHT, CHARLIE BROWN.. YOU'D BETTER WATCH HIM..

WELL, WHAT DO YOU THINK? SHALL I GIVE HIM THE OL' CHANGE OF PACE? THE LET-UP?

NO, HE'D KILL IT, CHARLIE BROWN...JUST GIVE HIM FAST ONES, BUT KEEP THEM LOW..

THIS GUY SAYS FOR ME TO TELL YOU THAT IF YOU THROW ANYTHING THAT EVEN **LOOKS** LIKE IT MIGHT BE A BEAN-BALL, HE'S GOING TO COME OUT HERE AND POUND YOU RIGHT INTO THE GROUND!

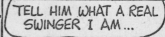

YOU SAY YOU MET THIS LINUS KID AT CAMP?

YES, AND THE YEAR BEFORE I MET A FRIEND OF HIS NAMED CHARLIE BROWN..

HE WAS A STRANGE ROUND-HEADED KID WHO NEVER TALKED ABOUT ANYTHING EXCEPT BASEBALL AND THIS AWFUL TEAM OF HIS THAT ALWAYS LOSES...

I LOVE BASEBALL! GET ON THE PHONE, QUICK! TELL HIM YOUR FRIEND, "PEPPERMINT" PATTY, HAS VOLUNTEERED TO HELP!

I REALLY LOVE BASEBALL! I'LL TAKE OVER THIS KID'S TEAM, AND SHOW HIM HOW TO **WIN**!!

"PEPPERMINT" PATTY, THIS IS SNOOPY, OUR SHORTSTOP..

GLAD TO KNOW YA, PAL!

NOW, IF YOU'LL COME OVER HERE, I'LL INTRODUCE YOU TO LUCY AND SOME OF THE OTHER GIRLS...

Y'KNOW WHAT?

THAT SHORTSTOP IS THE FUNNIEST LOOKIN' KID I'VE EVER SEEN!

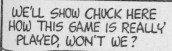

HI! I HEAR YOU'RE MY CATCHER..

WELL, WE WON'T NEED ANY SIGNALS...I'LL JUST FOG IT BY 'EM, AND YOU CATCH 'EM, OKAY? BY THE WAY, WHAT WAS THAT YOU WERE WHISTLING?

JUST A LITTLE SOMETHING BY BEETHOVEN

OH...

I COME CLEAR ACROSS TOWN TO PLAY BALL, AND WHO DO I GET FOR A CATCHER? A MINIATURE LEONARD BERNSTEIN!

And don't forget about all the other PEANUTS books in CORONET Book editions. Good Grief! More than THREE MILLION of them in paperback! See the check-list overleaf.

© 1970 United Feature Syndicate, Inc.

Wherever Paperbacks Are Sold

SNOOPYOLOGY

All these books are available at your bookshop or newsagent, or can be ordered direct from the publisher. Just tick the titles you want and fill in the form below.

....

CORONET BOOKS, P.O. Box 11, Falmouth, Cornwall.

Please send cheque or postal order. No currency, and allow the following for postage and packing:
1 book – 7p per copy, 2–4 books – 5p per copy, 5–8 books – 4p per copy, 9–15 books – 2½p per copy, 16–30 books – 2p per copy in U.K., 7p per copy overseas.

Name ....

Address ....

....